I0017399

THEORY
OF SUPPLY

Freelance Money: A Freelancer's Guide to Diverse Income Streams

Table of Contents

Grant Writing: Assist non-profits, startups, or research organizations in securing funding by offering your expertise in grant proposal writing.

Social Media Content: Offer your services to create engaging and shareable content for various social media platforms, helping businesses connect with their audience.

eBook Creation: Partner with authors or businesses to turn their ideas into eBooks, covering a wide range of topics from self-help to niche industry insights.

Freelance Journalism: Write articles for online magazines, newspapers, or news websites on topics that interest you and align with your expertise.

Resume and Cover Letter Writing: Help individuals enhance their professional image by crafting compelling resumes and cover letters that stand out to potential employers.

Scriptwriting for Videos or Podcasts: Explore opportunities in creating scripts for video content on platforms like YouTube or podcasts, offering a unique storytelling perspective.

Introduction

Embark on a journey of creative entrepreneurship with "Freelance Money: A Freelancer's Guide to Diverse Income Streams." This comprehensive guide delves into ten distinct avenues where freelancers can not only monetize their skills but also discover fulfilling paths in the ever-evolving landscape of the gig economy.

Explore the art of Freelance Writing and unlock the potential to make money by creating engaging content for diverse clients. Dive into the world of Content Creation, SEO-Optimized Articles, Technical Writing, Copywriting for Marketing, Grant Writing, and Social Media Content, discovering strategies to stand out in each specialized field.

Unlock the secrets of eBook Creation, where freelancers can partner with authors or businesses to transform ideas into digital masterpieces. The book also navigates the landscape of Freelance Journalism, offering insights into how writers can contribute impactful stories to online magazines and news websites.

Discover the art of crafting Social Media Gold, where freelancers create engaging content for various platforms, connecting businesses with their audiences. Finally, immerse yourself in the world of Scriptwriting for Videos or Podcasts, exploring opportunities to offer a unique storytelling perspective in the dynamic realms of digital content creation.

This book provides practical tips, real-world examples, and actionable strategies to help freelancers diversify their income streams, build a strong online presence, and turn their passion for writing and storytelling into a sustainable and fulfilling career.

Whether you're a seasoned freelancer or just starting, "Freelance Money: A Freelancer's Guide to Diverse Income Streams" is your go-to guide for navigating the exciting and ever-expanding landscape of freelance opportunities.

Unlocking Income Streams: Making Money through Freelance Content Creation for Blogs

In today's digital age, where online presence is paramount for businesses and individuals alike, the demand for engaging and informative blog content is at an all-time high. Freelance writers can capitalize on this trend by offering their services to those seeking to boost their online presence through well-crafted blog posts. In this article, we will explore the various ways you can monetize your writing skills and create a sustainable income stream as a freelance blog content creator.

Understanding the Landscape:

Before delving into the strategies for making money through blog content creation, it's crucial to understand the current landscape of online content. Businesses, entrepreneurs, and even individuals are constantly vying for attention in the vast digital space. High-quality blog content serves as a powerful tool to attract, engage, and retain an audience. This demand creates an opportunity for freelance writers to position themselves as valuable assets in the content creation ecosystem.

Building a Niche Expertise:

To stand out in the competitive world of freelance writing, consider specializing in a niche. Whether it's technology, lifestyle, finance, or any other area of interest, having a niche expertise enhances your credibility and makes you more attractive to potential clients. Businesses often prefer writers who understand their industry and can create content that resonates with their target audience.

Creating an Online Portfolio:

Establishing a strong online presence is crucial for any freelance writer. Develop a professional website or use platforms like LinkedIn to showcase your writing portfolio. Include samples of your best blog posts, highlighting your versatility and expertise in different topics. A well-curated portfolio serves as a virtual resume, making it easier for potential clients to assess your skills and suitability for their projects.

Networking and Marketing:

In the freelancing world, networking is key. Connect with businesses, entrepreneurs, and fellow freelancers through social media platforms, online forums, and networking events. Actively participate in discussions, share your expertise, and showcase your passion for creating compelling content. Word of mouth and referrals often play a significant role in securing freelance writing opportunities.

Additionally, invest time in marketing your services. Utilize social media to share snippets of your work, offer valuable insights related to your niche, and engage with potential clients. A well-executed marketing strategy can help you attract clients actively seeking freelance writers for their blog content needs.

Setting Competitive Rates:

Determining your pricing strategy is a crucial aspect of making money as a freelance blog content creator. Research industry standards, consider your level of expertise, and factor in the time and effort required for each project. While it's important to set competitive rates, don't undervalue your skills. Quality content often commands higher prices, and clients are willing to pay for value.

Exploring Content Platforms:

Consider leveraging content platforms and marketplaces to find potential clients. Websites like Upwork, Freelancer, and Fiverr connect freelancers with clients seeking content creation services. Create a compelling profile, showcase your skills, and actively bid on relevant projects. These platforms provide a convenient way to find clients and build a diverse portfolio.

Offering Additional Services:

To diversify your income streams, consider offering additional services beyond blog content creation. This could include social media management, content strategy consulting, or even providing insights on optimizing blog posts for search engines (SEO). By expanding your service offerings, you position yourself as a comprehensive solution for clients looking to enhance their overall online presence.

Delivering Consistent Quality:

Building a sustainable freelance career hinges on consistently delivering high-quality content. Meet deadlines, communicate effectively with clients, and be open to feedback. Satisfied clients are more likely to become repeat customers and may even refer you to others in their network. Building a positive reputation is invaluable in the freelancing world.

Investing in Continuous Learning:

The digital landscape is ever-evolving, and staying updated on industry trends and best practices is essential for long-term success. Invest time in continuous learning, whether it's through online courses, webinars, or networking with other professionals in your niche. Adapting to new trends and technologies ensures that your skills remain relevant and in-demand.

Conclusion:

Freelance content creation for blogs presents a lucrative opportunity for writers to monetize their skills and contribute to the ever-expanding world of online content. By building a niche expertise, creating a strong online presence, networking effectively, and delivering consistent quality, freelancers can establish themselves as valuable assets in the digital landscape. Embrace the dynamic nature of the industry, stay committed to excellence, and watch as your freelance writing endeavors turn into a rewarding and sustainable source of income.

Mastering the Art of Monetization: Making Money with SEO-Optimized Articles

In the ever-expanding digital realm, where the battle for online visibility is fierce, businesses are increasingly turning to SEO-optimized content to enhance their website's visibility. For freelance writers, specializing in creating content that is not only well-written but also optimized for search engines presents a golden opportunity to monetize their skills. In this article, we will delve into the strategies and techniques that can help you make money by offering SEO-optimized articles to clients eager to boost their online presence.

Understanding the Power of SEO:

Search Engine Optimization (SEO) is the cornerstone of online visibility. Businesses strive to rank higher on search engine results pages (SERPs) to attract organic traffic. Well-optimized content is a powerful tool in achieving this goal, as it not only provides valuable information but also aligns with the algorithms that search engines use to determine rankings.

Building Your SEO Expertise:

To capitalize on the demand for SEO-optimized content, it's crucial to build your expertise in SEO principles and practices. Stay updated on search engine algorithms, keyword research, and on-page optimization techniques. Understanding how search engines work will empower you to create content that not only resonates with the audience but also meets the criteria that search engines prioritize.

Conducting Comprehensive Keyword Research:

Keywords are the foundation of SEO-optimized content. Invest time in conducting thorough keyword research to identify relevant terms and phrases that potential clients want to target. Tools like Google Keyword Planner, SEMrush, and Ahrefs can aid in uncovering high-impact keywords related to your client's industry or niche.

Crafting Compelling, Relevant Content:

SEO-optimized content is not just about stuffing keywords; it's about creating high-quality, relevant, and engaging content that adds value to the reader. Develop the ability to seamlessly integrate keywords into your writing while maintaining a natural flow. Strive to answer the reader's queries, provide solutions, and deliver content that keeps them engaged throughout.

Optimizing Meta Tags and Descriptions:

Beyond the body of the content, pay attention to optimizing meta tags and descriptions. Craft compelling meta titles and descriptions that not only include relevant keywords but also entice users to click through to the website. These elements play a crucial role in improving click-through rates and, subsequently, a website's overall visibility.

Utilizing SEO Tools:

Embrace the array of SEO tools available to streamline your optimization efforts. Tools like Yoast SEO, Moz, and Google Analytics can provide valuable insights into your content's performance, keyword effectiveness, and user behavior. Leveraging these tools not only enhances your efficiency but also allows you to demonstrate tangible results to clients.

Offering Comprehensive SEO Packages:

To maximize your revenue, consider offering comprehensive SEO packages that go beyond individual articles. Bundle services such as keyword research, on-page optimization, and regular content updates to provide clients with a holistic SEO strategy. This approach positions you as a one-stop solution for businesses aiming to improve their online visibility.

Showcasing SEO Success Stories:

Create a portfolio highlighting the success stories of your SEO-optimized content. Demonstrate how your work has contributed to improved search engine rankings, increased organic traffic, and enhanced online visibility for your clients. Case studies and testimonials from satisfied clients add credibility to your services and attract new business.

Networking with Digital Marketing Professionals:

Establish connections with digital marketing professionals and agencies. Collaborate with SEO experts, web developers, and marketing strategists to expand your network and tap into a broader pool of potential clients. Networking within the digital marketing community can open doors to lucrative opportunities and collaborations.

Staying Informed about SEO Trends:

The world of SEO is dynamic, with constant updates and evolving trends. Stay informed about the latest changes in search engine algorithms, emerging SEO techniques, and industry best practices. Proactively adapting to these changes ensures that your SEO-optimized content remains effective and aligned with current standards.

Setting Competitive Pricing:

Determining the right pricing strategy is crucial for monetizing your SEO-optimized content services. Consider factors such as the level of competition, the complexity of the project, and the value you bring to your clients. While offering competitive rates, emphasize the long-term benefits of well-optimized content in driving organic traffic and improving search engine rankings.

Conclusion:

In the digital age, where online visibility is a make-or-break factor for businesses, the demand for SEO-optimized content continues to rise. Freelance writers can seize this opportunity by mastering the art of creating content that not only meets high-quality standards but also aligns with SEO principles. By building expertise, conducting thorough keyword research, and staying updated on industry trends, you can position yourself as a valuable asset in the world of SEO-optimized content creation. Embrace the dynamic nature of SEO, continuously refine your skills, and watch as your freelance endeavors transform into a lucrative venture, helping clients enhance their website's visibility and driving success in the digital landscape.

Navigating the Path to Success: Making Money through Technical Writing

In the ever-evolving landscape of technology, healthcare, and finance, the demand for clear and concise documentation is on the rise. Technical writing has emerged as a critical skill, with companies seeking professionals who can craft manuals, guides, and documentation that bridge the gap between complexity and understanding. For freelance writers, this presents a lucrative opportunity to explore and monetize their expertise in technical writing. In this article, we will delve into the various ways you can make money by offering technical writing services to companies in diverse industries.

Understanding the Role of Technical Writing:

Technical writing involves translating complex information into clear and accessible content. Whether it's creating user manuals, product guides, or technical documentation, the goal is to provide information that is easily comprehensible for the intended audience. This skill is highly valued across industries where precise communication is essential.

Identifying Niche Industries:

Explore opportunities in niche industries such as technology, healthcare, and finance. Each sector has unique requirements for technical documentation, and by specializing in one or more of these areas, you can position yourself as an expert in crafting content tailored to the specific needs and intricacies of that industry.

Creating Comprehensive User Manuals:

Companies often require user manuals for their products or services. Develop the skill to create comprehensive and user-friendly manuals that guide individuals through the functionalities and features of a product. Your ability to simplify complex information while maintaining accuracy will make your technical writing services invaluable to companies producing intricate products.

Crafting In-Depth Guides:

In addition to user manuals, there is a growing demand for in-depth guides that delve into specific topics or processes. Whether it's a guide on implementing a new technology solution or navigating complex financial procedures, your expertise in crafting clear, step-by-step guides can position you as a go-to resource for companies seeking thorough documentation.

Exploring Healthcare Documentation:

The healthcare industry relies heavily on precise documentation, from patient care manuals to medical device instructions. Familiarize yourself with the regulatory standards and compliance requirements within the healthcare sector. Offering services that align with these standards can make your technical writing skills indispensable to healthcare organizations.

Understanding Financial Procedures:

In the finance industry, where accuracy and clarity are paramount, technical writing plays a crucial role. Create documentation that explains complex financial procedures, compliance regulations, or investment strategies in a way that is accessible to a diverse audience. Your ability to simplify financial jargon can make you a sought-after resource for financial institutions and companies.

Building a Professional Portfolio:

Develop a professional portfolio showcasing your expertise in technical writing. Include samples of user manuals, guides, and documentation you have created for past clients. Highlight any industry-specific knowledge you possess, demonstrating your ability to understand and communicate complex information in a clear and concise manner.

Utilizing Online Platforms:

Explore freelancing platforms such as Upwork, Freelancer, or Fiverr to connect with businesses in need of technical writing services. Create a compelling profile that emphasizes your experience, expertise, and the industries you specialize in. Actively bid on relevant projects and use these platforms as a means to build a diverse portfolio and client base.

Networking with Industry Professionals:

Build connections with professionals in the industries you target. Attend industry-specific events, join online forums, and engage with professionals who may require technical writing services. Networking with individuals already immersed in these industries can open doors to lucrative opportunities and long-term collaborations.

Offering Consultation Services:

Go beyond creating documentation by offering consultation services. Provide insights on best practices for creating effective technical documentation, offer guidance on compliance standards, and help companies streamline their communication processes. Positioning

17

yourself as a consultant in addition to a writer adds another layer of value to your services.

Setting Competitive Rates:

Determining your pricing strategy is crucial for success in technical writing. Consider factors such as the complexity of the project, the level of expertise required, and the industry standards. While offering competitive rates, emphasize the long-term benefits of well-crafted technical documentation in enhancing user experience, reducing support costs, and ensuring regulatory compliance.

Conclusion:

Technical writing is a dynamic field with vast opportunities for freelance writers to make a substantial income. By honing your skills in crafting user manuals, guides, and documentation for industries like technology, healthcare, or finance, you position yourself as a valuable asset to businesses seeking clear and precise communication. Build a professional portfolio, leverage online platforms, network with industry professionals, and offer comprehensive services to stand out in the competitive world of technical writing. Embrace the challenges and intricacies of each industry you target, and watch as your technical writing endeavors evolve into a rewarding and sustainable source of income.

The Art of Persuasion: Unlocking Income Opportunities through Copywriting for Marketing

In the digital age, where attention spans are fleeting and competition for consumer attention is fierce, the role of persuasive writing has never been more crucial. For freelance writers, specializing in copywriting for marketing opens up a realm of opportunities to make money by crafting compelling copy for advertisements, product descriptions, and various marketing materials. In this article, we will explore the strategies and techniques that can help you monetize your skills in persuasive writing and create a lucrative income stream.

Understanding the Essence of Copywriting for Marketing:

Copywriting for marketing is more than just words on a page; it's a strategic art form designed to influence, engage, and ultimately persuade the audience to take a desired action. Whether it's convincing them to make a purchase, sign up for a newsletter, or click a link, effective copywriting is at the heart of successful marketing campaigns.

Developing Persuasive Writing Skills:

To embark on a successful journey in copywriting for marketing, focus on developing your persuasive writing skills. Understand the psychology of persuasion, the nuances of consumer behavior, and the principles that drive effective communication. Mastering the art of crafting messages that resonate with your target audience is the key to becoming a sought-after copywriter.

Creating Compelling Advertisements:

Advertisements are a powerful vehicle for conveying a message in a concise yet impactful manner. Develop the ability to distill complex ideas into compelling, attention-grabbing ad copy. Whether it's for social media, online banners, or traditional print, your copywriting skills should evoke emotions, pique curiosity, and drive the audience to take action.

Crafting Irresistible Product Descriptions:

Product descriptions serve as the virtual salesperson for online businesses. Your copywriting prowess can turn mundane product details into a compelling narrative that entices customers to make a purchase. Focus on highlighting the unique selling points, benefits, and the value proposition of the product in a way that resonates with the target audience.

Optimizing Copy for Search Engines (SEO):

In the digital landscape, search engine optimization (SEO) is integral to the success of marketing efforts. Integrate SEO principles into your copywriting by strategically incorporating relevant keywords. This not only enhances the visibility of your content but also ensures that your persuasive copy reaches a wider audience through search engine results.

Understanding the Target Audience:

Effective copywriting begins with a deep understanding of the target audience. Conduct thorough research to identify the demographics, preferences, and pain points of the audience you are writing for. Tailor your copy to resonate with their needs, desires, and aspirations, creating a connection that fosters trust and engagement.

Diversifying Your Copywriting Services:

To maximize your income potential, consider diversifying your copywriting services. Offer a range of services including website copy, email campaigns, social media posts, and video scripts. Different platforms and mediums require distinct approaches, and by mastering various formats, you position yourself as a versatile and in-demand copywriter.

Building a Strong Portfolio:

As a freelance copywriter, your portfolio is your showcase of skills. Compile a portfolio that highlights your best work across different industries and formats. Include examples of successful campaigns, before-and-after transformations, and metrics demonstrating the impact of your persuasive writing. A compelling portfolio serves as a powerful marketing tool to attract potential clients.

Networking in Marketing Circles:

Networking is a cornerstone of success in the freelance world. Engage with marketing professionals, business owners, and fellow copywriters. Attend industry events, join online forums, and actively participate in discussions. Building relationships with individuals in the marketing sphere can lead to collaborations, referrals, and lucrative opportunities.

Utilizing Freelance Platforms and Agencies:

Freelance platforms like Upwork, Freelancer, and Fiverr are bustling marketplaces where businesses seek copywriting services. Create a compelling profile, showcase your expertise, and actively bid on relevant projects. Additionally, consider collaborating with marketing agencies that often require freelance copywriters to complement their team's efforts.

Continual Learning and Adaptation:

The marketing landscape is dynamic, with trends and consumer behaviors evolving constantly. Stay informed about the latest developments in marketing, copywriting techniques, and emerging platforms. Continual learning and adaptation ensure that your copy remains relevant, effective, and aligned with the ever-changing needs of the digital marketplace.

Setting Competitive Rates:

Determining your pricing strategy is a crucial aspect of making money as a freelance copywriter. Research industry standards, consider the complexity of the project, and factor in your level of expertise. While offering competitive rates, emphasize the return on investment that businesses can expect from your persuasive copy in terms of increased conversions and engagement.

Conclusion:

Copywriting for marketing is a powerful avenue for freelance writers to monetize their persuasive writing skills. By mastering the art of creating compelling copy for advertisements, product descriptions, and marketing materials, you position yourself as a valuable asset in the digital landscape. Develop your persuasive writing skills, diversify your services, build a strong portfolio, and leverage networking opportunities to unlock a steady stream of income. As businesses continue to recognize the importance of persuasive communication in their marketing strategies, the demand for skilled copywriters is bound to grow, providing ample opportunities for freelancers to thrive in the exciting world of persuasive writing for marketing.

Unveiling the Power of Pen and Purpose: Making Money through Grant Writing

In the realm of freelancing, grant writing stands out as a unique and rewarding avenue for those who possess the skill to weave compelling narratives with a mission-driven focus. Grant writers play a pivotal role in assisting non-profits, startups, and research organizations in securing essential funding for their projects. In this article, we'll explore the strategies and nuances that can help you monetize your expertise in grant writing, transforming your passion for impactful storytelling into a lucrative income stream.

Understanding the Significance of Grant Writing:

Grant writing is more than just stringing words together; it's a strategic and purposeful craft that aims to secure financial support for organizations with a mission. Non-profits, startups, and research organizations often rely on grants to fund their initiatives, and grant writers serve as the architects of proposals that articulate the organization's vision and impact.

Developing Expertise in Grant Proposal Writing:

To embark on a successful career in grant writing, it's essential to develop expertise in crafting compelling grant proposals. This involves understanding the intricacies of grant applications, conducting thorough research on potential funding sources, and tailoring proposals to align with the specific criteria and priorities of grant-making entities.

Navigating the Grant Landscape:

The grant landscape is diverse, encompassing various sectors such as education, healthcare, environmental conservation, and social justice. Identify the areas that align with your interests and expertise, allowing you to specialize in specific niches. By understanding the unique challenges and opportunities within a particular sector, you can offer more targeted and effective grant writing services.

Assisting Non-Profits in Achieving Their Mission:

Non-profit organizations, driven by a commitment to social impact, often lack the resources to hire in-house grant writers. Freelancers can bridge this gap by offering their grant writing expertise to help non-profits secure funding for their projects. Whether it's funding for community development, healthcare initiatives, or educational programs, grant writers play a crucial role in supporting non-profits in achieving their mission-driven goals.

Empowering Startups to Flourish:

Startups, especially in their early stages, may struggle to attract investors or secure traditional funding. Grant writing provides an alternative avenue for startups to access much-needed capital. As a grant writer, you can assist startups in navigating grant opportunities that align with their business model and objectives, helping them gain a foothold in their respective industries.

Fostering Research and Innovation:

Research organizations rely on grants to fuel groundbreaking projects and scientific advancements. Grant writers contribute to the success of research initiatives by effectively communicating the significance and potential impact of the proposed studies. As a grant writer, you become an essential collaborator in bringing research visions to life by securing the necessary funding.

Building a Professional Portfolio:

A compelling portfolio is your ticket to success in the world of grant writing. Showcase successful grant proposals you've crafted, highlighting the outcomes and impact they've had on the organizations you've worked with. Include testimonials from satisfied clients, illustrating your ability to effectively communicate their mission and secure funding.

Networking with Organizations and Foundations:

Networking is a cornerstone of success in grant writing. Establish connections with non-profits, startups, and research organizations seeking funding. Attend industry conferences, workshops, and virtual events to engage with potential clients. Additionally, build relationships with foundations and grant-making entities to stay informed about new opportunities and requirements.

Utilizing Online Platforms:

Freelance platforms such as Upwork, Freelancer, and Fiverr provide a digital marketplace for grant writers to connect with organizations in need of funding support. Create a compelling profile that highlights your expertise, experience, and success stories. Actively bid on relevant projects and leverage these platforms to build a diverse client base.

Offering Grant Writing Workshops and Consultations:

Beyond crafting grant proposals, consider offering workshops and consultations to organizations looking to enhance their grant writing skills. Share your expertise on best practices, tips for successful applications, and strategies to stand out in a competitive grant landscape. This additional service adds value to your offerings and positions you as a comprehensive resource for organizations seeking funding.

Setting Competitive Rates:

Determining your pricing strategy is crucial in grant writing. Consider the complexity of the project, the amount of research involved, and the level of detail required. While offering competitive rates, emphasize the long-term benefits of successful grant acquisition, such as increased project funding and organizational growth.

Continual Professional Development:

The grant landscape is dynamic, with evolving trends, requirements, and priorities. Stay informed about changes in funding priorities, emerging grant opportunities, and shifts in the philanthropic landscape. Continuous professional development ensures that your grant writing skills remain sharp and relevant, enhancing your ability to secure funding for your clients.

Conclusion:

Grant writing is a potent blend of storytelling, strategy, and social impact. As a freelance grant writer, you have the opportunity to make a significant difference by assisting non-profits, startups, and research organizations in securing the funding they need to bring their visions to fruition. Develop your expertise, build a strong portfolio, network with organizations and foundations, and utilize online platforms to unlock a steady stream of grant writing opportunities. By transforming your passion for impactful storytelling into a lucrative profession, you not only empower organizations to thrive but also carve out a fulfilling and meaningful career in the dynamic world of grant writing.

The Art and Business of Crafting Social Media Gold: Monetizing Your Talent in Social Media Content Creation

In an era dominated by the digital landscape, the power of social media to shape narratives, engage audiences, and drive business success is undeniable. For freelance creators, the demand for captivating social media content is a goldmine waiting to be explored. In this article, we will delve into the strategies and methods to turn your passion for creating engaging and shareable content into a lucrative venture, helping businesses connect with their audience across various social media platforms.

Understanding the Impact of Social Media Content:

Social media has become an integral part of our daily lives, influencing opinions, shaping trends, and connecting people globally. For businesses, establishing a strong presence on social platforms is crucial for brand visibility, customer engagement, and ultimately, driving sales. Engaging and shareable content is the currency of success in the digital realm.

Developing Creative and Strategic Social Media Content:

As a social media content creator, your primary goal is to craft content that not only captures attention but also resonates with the target audience. Understand the demographics, preferences, and behaviors of the audience on each platform. Develop a creative and strategic approach to content creation that aligns with the brand's identity and goals.

Identifying Your Niche and Expertise:

Social media is diverse, and each platform caters to different types of content. Identify your niche and expertise – whether it's visual content on Instagram, short-form videos on TikTok, or professional updates on LinkedIn. Focusing on a specific niche allows you to hone your skills and stand out in a crowded digital landscape.

Building a Strong Portfolio:

Your portfolio is your digital storefront. Showcase your best work across various social media platforms, illustrating your ability to create content that engages, informs, and entertains. Include metrics such as engagement rates, follower growth, or reach to provide tangible evidence of the impact your content has on the audience.

Utilizing Your Unique Voice and Style:

Developing a unique voice and style sets you apart in the competitive world of social media content creation. Whether it's a distinctive writing style, a particular aesthetic, or a signature way of storytelling, your individuality becomes your brand. Clients are drawn to creators who bring something fresh and authentic to the table.

Leveraging Video Content:

Video content has become a dominant force in social media. From short-form videos on platforms like TikTok and Instagram Reels to long-form content on YouTube, video is a versatile and engaging medium. Invest in developing your video creation skills, including editing and storytelling, to offer a comprehensive range of content creation services.

Understanding Each Social Media Platform:

Each social media platform has its own dynamics, algorithms, and user behavior. Understand the nuances of platforms like Instagram, Facebook, Twitter, LinkedIn, TikTok, and others. Tailor your content strategy to fit the specific characteristics of each platform, maximizing reach and engagement for your clients.

Providing Consistent and Valuable Content:

Consistency is key in social media content creation. Develop a content calendar that ensures a steady stream of posts aligned with your client's goals and audience expectations. Delivering valuable content – whether it's educational, entertaining, or inspiring – keeps the audience engaged and encourages them to share the content with their networks.

Networking and Collaboration:

Networking is an essential element of success in the freelance world. Connect with businesses, influencers, and fellow content creators in your niche. Collaborate on projects, participate in challenges, and engage in discussions. Building a network not only opens doors to potential clients but also enhances your visibility within the social media community.

Utilizing Freelance Platforms and Social Media Management Tools:

Freelance platforms such as Upwork or Fiverr offer a platform to showcase your social media content creation services. Create a compelling profile that highlights your skills, expertise, and successful projects. Additionally, leverage social media management tools like Buffer, Hootsuite, or Sprout Social to streamline your workflow and effectively manage multiple clients.

Offering Additional Services:

Diversify your income streams by offering additional services beyond content creation. This could include social media strategy consulting, analytics reporting, or managing advertising campaigns. Providing a comprehensive suite of services positions you as a valuable partner for businesses seeking to enhance their overall social media presence.

Setting Competitive Rates:

Determining your pricing strategy is crucial in the freelance world. Consider factors such as your level of expertise, the complexity of the project, and the value you bring to your clients. While offering competitive rates, emphasize the long-term benefits of engaging and shareable content in building brand awareness, increasing engagement, and driving business growth.

Staying Updated on Social Media Trends:

The social media landscape is ever-evolving, with trends and features constantly changing. Stay updated on the latest trends, algorithm updates, and emerging features on various platforms.

Being at the forefront of social media trends allows you to offer innovative and impactful content that resonates with current audience preferences.

Conclusion:

Social media content creation is not just an art; it's a thriving business opportunity for freelance creators. By developing your skills, understanding the nuances of each platform, and offering a range of services, you can turn your passion for creating engaging and shareable content into a lucrative career. Building a strong portfolio, networking with industry professionals, and staying updated on social media trends are essential steps toward establishing yourself as a sought-after social media content creator. As businesses increasingly recognize the importance of a vibrant social media presence, the demand for skilled content creators is set to grow, providing ample opportunities for freelancers to carve a successful and fulfilling path in the dynamic world of social media content creation.

Transforming Ideas into Profit: A Guide to Making Money through eBook Creation

In the ever-expanding digital landscape, eBooks have emerged as powerful tools for sharing knowledge, telling stories, and disseminating valuable information. For freelance writers and creatives, there lies a unique opportunity to monetize their skills by partnering with authors or businesses to turn their ideas into eBooks.

This article will explore the strategies and methods to embark on a successful journey in eBook creation, covering a diverse range of topics from self-help to niche industry insights.

Understanding the eBook Landscape:

eBooks have become a popular medium for individuals and businesses to share their expertise, stories, and unique insights with a global audience. With the rise of digital platforms, self-publishing, and the widespread use of eReaders, the eBook industry has seen tremendous growth. This presents a golden opportunity for freelancers to offer their eBook creation services to those looking to turn their ideas into tangible and marketable digital products.

Identifying Potential Collaborators:

To kickstart your journey into eBook creation, start by identifying potential collaborators. Authors, entrepreneurs, professionals, and businesses often have valuable ideas and insights that can be transformed into eBooks. Seek out individuals or organizations aligned with your interests or expertise, whether it's in the realm of self-help, business, technology, or any niche industry.

Crafting a Compelling Pitch:

Once you've identified potential collaborators, craft a compelling pitch that outlines the value you bring to the eBook creation process. Highlight your writing skills, understanding of the target audience, and the ability to turn ideas into engaging and cohesive narratives. Clearly articulate the benefits of collaborating with you in transforming their vision into a professionally crafted eBook.

Building a Niche Expertise:

Specializing in a niche can enhance your credibility and attract collaborators with specific needs. Whether it's wellness, finance, technology, or any other area of interest, having a niche expertise allows you to tailor your services to a particular audience. This not only makes your pitch more appealing but also positions you as a go-to expert in your chosen field.

Creating a Collaborative Process:

Establish a collaborative process that ensures smooth communication and efficient workflow between you and your collaborators. Clearly define the scope of work, timelines, and expectations. Foster an environment where ideas can be exchanged freely, and revisions can be made collaboratively to create the best possible eBook.

Offering a Comprehensive Service Package:

To maximize your income potential, consider offering a comprehensive service package beyond just writing. Include services such as editing, formatting, cover design, and even assistance with the self-publishing process. Providing an end-to-end solution makes your services more attractive to collaborators who may prefer a hassle-free experience.

Developing a Professional Portfolio:

A strong portfolio is crucial in showcasing your capabilities and attracting potential collaborators. Include samples of previous eBook projects, emphasizing your ability to adapt to different genres and writing styles. If possible, gather testimonials from satisfied collaborators to add credibility and demonstrate the positive impact of your work.

Utilizing Self-Publishing Platforms:

Take advantage of self-publishing platforms like Amazon Kindle Direct Publishing (KDP), Apple Books, and others. Familiarize yourself with the submission guidelines and publishing processes on these platforms. Offering to handle the technical aspects of self-publishing can be an added value for your collaborators, streamlining the process for them.

Networking within Writing and Publishing Communities:

Networking is pivotal in the freelance world. Engage with writers, authors, and professionals in the publishing industry. Join online forums, attend writing conferences, and participate in discussions related to eBook creation and self-publishing. Building relationships within these communities can lead to valuable collaborations and referrals.

Setting Competitive Pricing:

Determining your pricing strategy requires a balance between the complexity of the project, your level of expertise, and the value you provide. Research industry standards for eBook creation services and consider offering different pricing packages based on the scope of work. Clearly communicate the value proposition to potential collaborators.

Leveraging Social Media and Online Presence:

Establish a strong online presence to attract potential collaborators. Utilize social media platforms, create a professional website showcasing your services, and share valuable insights related to eBook creation. Engage with your audience, participate in relevant conversations, and showcase your expertise to build credibility within the digital space.

Keeping Abreast of Publishing Trends:

The publishing landscape is continually evolving, with new trends and technologies influencing how eBooks are created and consumed. Stay informed about industry trends, emerging technologies, and changes in reader preferences. Adapting to these trends ensures that your eBook creation services remain relevant and appealing to collaborators.

Continual Learning and Skill Enhancement:

Invest time in continual learning to enhance your writing skills, stay updated on industry best practices, and explore new writing techniques. Consider taking courses on eBook formatting, cover design, or marketing to broaden your skill set and offer a more comprehensive service to your collaborators.

Conclusion:

Embarking on a journey to make money through eBook creation offers freelancers a rewarding and diverse path. By partnering with authors or businesses to turn their ideas into eBooks, you not only monetize your writing skills but also contribute to the dissemination of valuable knowledge and stories. Craft compelling pitches, build a niche expertise, offer comprehensive service packages, and leverage self-publishing platforms to showcase your work. Networking within writing and publishing communities, maintaining a strong online presence, and staying updated on industry trends are key elements in establishing a successful eBook creation business. As the demand for unique and engaging content continues to rise, freelancers in the eBook creation space find themselves at the intersection.

The Freelance Journalist's Guide to Turning Passion into Profit

In the dynamic landscape of digital media, freelance journalism has emerged as a thriving avenue for writers to share their expertise, tell compelling stories, and, importantly, make money doing what they love. Writing articles for online magazines, newspapers, or news websites provides freelancers with the flexibility to choose topics that align with their interests and expertise. In this article, we will explore the strategies and methods to monetize your skills as a freelance journalist, turning your passion for writing into a lucrative venture.

Understanding the Freelance Journalism Landscape:

Freelance journalism offers a unique opportunity for writers to contribute to various publications without being tied to a full-time position. With the rise of online media platforms, the demand for high-quality and diverse content has never been higher. Freelancers can leverage their expertise and passion to write articles on topics ranging from current affairs and features to niche interests.

Identifying Your Niche and Expertise:

Before diving into freelance journalism, identify your niche and expertise. Consider your interests, experiences, and areas of knowledge that you are passionate about. Whether it's technology, health, lifestyle, or specific industries, having a defined niche allows you to target publications that align with your expertise and increases your chances of securing assignments.

Building a Diverse Portfolio:

Create a portfolio showcasing a diverse range of articles you have written. Include samples that demonstrate your versatility, covering different styles of journalism, such as news reporting, feature writing, interviews, and opinion pieces. A well-rounded portfolio not only showcases your skills but also allows potential clients to see the breadth of topics you can cover.

Pitching to Relevant Publications:

Research and identify publications that align with your niche and interests. Develop targeted pitches that are tailored to each publication's audience and style. Clearly articulate the value you bring as a freelance journalist, emphasizing your unique perspective and ability to deliver engaging and well-researched content. Personalized pitches increase your chances of grabbing the attention of editors.

Leveraging Freelance Platforms and Job Boards:

Explore freelance platforms and job boards that connect writers with opportunities. Platforms like Upwork, Freelancer, and LinkedIn often have job listings for freelance journalists. Create a compelling profile that highlights your experience, skills, and areas of expertise.

Actively apply to relevant gigs, and consider long-term collaborations with publications looking for consistent contributors.

Developing Strong Relationships with Editors:

Building strong relationships with editors is key to establishing a successful freelance journalism career. Deliver high-quality work consistently, meet deadlines, and be open to feedback. Editors appreciate reliability and professionalism, and establishing a positive rapport can lead to repeat assignments and recommendations to other publications.

Offering Editorial Services Beyond Writing:

Expand your service offerings by providing additional editorial services beyond writing. This could include copy editing, proofreading, and fact-checking. Offering a comprehensive package makes you a valuable resource for publications seeking not only engaging content but also a polished and error-free final product.

Creating Sponsored Content and Brand Collaborations:

Explore opportunities to create sponsored content and collaborate with brands. Some publications and websites work with freelance journalists to produce sponsored articles that integrate seamlessly with their regular content. This opens up new revenue streams and allows you to work with brands that align with your values and expertise.

Participating in Journalism Fellowships and Grants:

Apply for journalism fellowships and grants that support independent journalists. Many organizations and foundations offer funding opportunities for journalists working on impactful and investigative stories. Participating in fellowships not only provides financial support but also enhances your portfolio and credibility as a journalist.

Monetizing Your Personal Blog or Newsletter:

If you have a personal blog or newsletter, explore ways to monetize your platform. Offer premium content or subscriptions, engage in affiliate marketing, or collaborate with brands for sponsored content. Your blog or newsletter can serve as a showcase of your writing style and attract potential clients seeking your expertise.

Setting Competitive Rates:

Determining your pricing strategy is crucial in freelance journalism. Research industry standards, consider the complexity of the assignment, and factor in your level of expertise. While offering competitive rates, emphasize the value of your journalistic skills, research capabilities, and unique perspective in delivering high-quality content.

Diversifying Your Income Streams:

Diversify your income streams by exploring various avenues within freelance journalism. In addition to writing articles, consider offering media consulting, hosting webinars or workshops, or contributing to podcasts. Diversification not only adds stability to your income but also allows you to showcase your expertise in different formats.

Staying Informed about Industry Trends:

The media industry is ever-evolving, with new trends, technologies, and reader preferences shaping the landscape. Stay informed about industry trends, emerging storytelling formats, and changes in media consumption habits. Adapting to these trends ensures that your freelance journalism remains relevant and resonates with contemporary audiences.

Conclusion:

Freelance journalism provides a fulfilling and financially rewarding path for writers passionate about sharing stories and insights. By identifying your niche, building a diverse portfolio, and pitching to relevant publications, you can turn your passion for writing into a thriving freelance career. Leverage freelance platforms, build strong relationships with editors, and explore additional editorial services to enhance your offerings. As the digital media landscape continues to evolve, freelance journalists have unprecedented opportunities to contribute meaningful content, connect with diverse audiences, and monetize their skills in the dynamic and ever-expanding world of journalism.

Crafting Careers: A Guide to Monetizing Your Talent in Resume and Cover Letter Writing

In the competitive landscape of job hunting, where first impressions matter, the demand for professionally crafted resumes and cover letters has surged. Freelancers with a knack for words and an understanding of the job market have found a lucrative avenue in offering their expertise to help individuals enhance their professional image. In this article, we will explore the strategies and methods to make money through resume and cover letter writing, assisting individuals in standing out to potential employers and landing their dream jobs.

Understanding the Importance of Professional Resumes and Cover Letters:

A resume and cover letter are often the first points of contact between job seekers and potential employers. A well-crafted resume and cover letter not only highlight an individual's skills and experiences but also create a compelling narrative that captures the attention of hiring managers. As job seekers recognize the significance of making a strong first impression, the demand for professional resume and cover letter writing services has skyrocketed.

Developing Expertise in Resume and Cover Letter Writing:

Before delving into the business of resume and cover letter writing, it's crucial to develop expertise in this specialized skill. Understand the best practices for resume formatting, tailor-made for different industries and career levels. Stay updated on current trends in cover letter writing, emphasizing personalized and impactful communication. By honing your skills, you position yourself as a valuable resource for individuals seeking to optimize their job application materials.

Identifying Target Audiences and Niches:

Define your target audience and consider specializing in specific niches. Whether it's entry-level professionals, mid-career changers, or executives seeking C-suite roles, each demographic has unique needs. Additionally, you may choose to specialize in specific industries such as IT, healthcare, or finance. By tailoring your services to a particular audience or industry, you can create more personalized and effective resumes and cover letters.

Building a Professional Portfolio:

Create a professional portfolio showcasing examples of resumes and cover letters you've crafted. Ensure that your portfolio includes a variety of industries and career levels to demonstrate your versatility. Include before-and-after transformations to highlight the impact of your services on job seekers' professional image. A strong portfolio becomes a powerful marketing tool, instilling confidence in potential clients.

Offering Additional Services:

Diversify your services beyond resume and cover letter writing. Consider offering services such as LinkedIn profile optimization, interview coaching, and career counseling. Providing a comprehensive package enhances your value proposition and positions you as a one-stop solution for individuals navigating the job market. Additional services contribute to a holistic approach in boosting clients' professional success.

Utilizing Freelance Platforms and Job Boards:

Leverage freelance platforms like Upwork, Freelancer, and Fiverr to connect with individuals seeking resume and cover letter writing services. Create a compelling profile that highlights your expertise, showcases client testimonials, and includes samples of your work. Actively bid on relevant projects, and use these platforms to build a diverse client base.

Networking with Career Professionals and Job Seekers:

Networking is key in the freelance world, especially in resume and cover letter writing. Connect with career professionals, job seekers, and individuals working in human resources or recruitment. Attend industry events, join online forums, and actively participate in discussions. Building relationships within these networks can lead to valuable referrals and long-term collaborations.

Providing Consultation Services:

Go beyond resume and cover letter writing by offering consultation services. Provide insights on job market trends, share tips for effective job searching, and offer guidance on career development. Offering consultation services positions you as a career expert, adding value to your clients beyond the immediate need for a polished resume.

Setting Competitive Rates:

Determining your pricing strategy is crucial for success in resume and cover letter writing. Research industry standards, consider the complexity of the project, and factor in your level of expertise. While offering competitive rates, emphasize the long-term benefits of a professionally crafted resume in securing job opportunities and advancing clients' careers.

Creating Educational Resources:

Consider creating educational resources such as webinars, ebooks, or blog posts that provide insights into effective resume and cover letter writing. Sharing your expertise not only establishes you as an authority in the field but also attracts potential clients seeking to enhance their job application skills. Educational content contributes to your online presence and credibility.

Staying Updated on Job Market Trends:

The job market is dynamic, with trends, expectations, and recruitment processes constantly evolving. Stay informed about current job market trends, industry-specific requirements, and changes in resume and cover letter preferences. Adapting to these trends ensures that your services remain relevant and effective in helping clients navigate the competitive job market.

Continual Learning and Skill Enhancement:

Invest time in continual learning to stay ahead in resume and cover letter writing. Attend workshops, participate in professional development courses, and engage with industry experts to enhance your skills. Continual learning allows you to integrate the latest strategies and techniques into your services, ensuring that you provide cutting-edge solutions to your clients.

Conclusion:

Resume and cover letter writing is not just a skill; it's a pathway to helping individuals shape their professional futures.

Crafting Narratives for Success: Monetizing Your Talent in Scriptwriting for Videos or Podcasts

In the digital age of content consumption, video platforms like YouTube and the ever-growing world of podcasts have become powerful mediums for storytelling, education, and entertainment. As the demand for engaging content continues to rise, scriptwriting for videos and podcasts has emerged as a lucrative opportunity for talented writers to monetize their storytelling prowess. In this article, we will explore the strategies and methods to make money through scriptwriting, offering a unique narrative perspective for video content or podcast episodes.

Understanding the Impact of Scriptwriting in Digital Content:

Scriptwriting serves as the backbone of engaging video content on platforms like YouTube and compelling narratives in podcasts. A well-crafted script not only captures the audience's attention but also guides the flow of the content, ensuring a seamless and captivating experience. As content creators on these platforms recognize the value of powerful storytelling, the demand for skilled scriptwriters has soared.

Identifying Opportunities in Video and Podcast Genres:

Before delving into scriptwriting, it's essential to identify the genres and niches that align with your interests and expertise. Whether it's educational content, entertainment, storytelling, or a specific industry focus, each genre presents unique opportunities. Consider the target audience and tailor your scriptwriting services to cater to the content creators or podcasters seeking your narrative expertise.

Building a Strong Portfolio:

Create a compelling portfolio showcasing your scriptwriting skills. Include samples of scripts you've crafted, highlighting the diversity of genres and formats. If possible, collaborate with content creators or podcasters to turn your scripts into actual episodes or videos, showcasing your ability to translate ideas into engaging and visually appealing content.

Networking with Content Creators and Podcasters:

Networking is a pivotal aspect of success in scriptwriting. Connect with content creators on platforms like YouTube or podcasters in your chosen niche. Attend industry events, engage in online forums, and actively participate in discussions. Building relationships within these communities can lead to collaborations, referrals, and long-term partnerships.

Pitching to Content Creators and Podcasters:

Craft targeted pitches to showcase your scriptwriting services to content creators and podcasters. Highlight your storytelling skills, understanding of the target audience, and the ability to create scripts that align with the creator's vision. Personalize your pitches to address the unique needs and preferences of each potential collaborator.

Utilizing Freelance Platforms and Job Boards:

Freelance platforms like Upwork, Freelancer, and Fiverr provide opportunities to connect with content creators and podcasters seeking scriptwriting services. Create a compelling profile that emphasizes your expertise, includes samples of your work, and showcases client testimonials. Actively bid on relevant projects, offering your unique storytelling perspective.

Offering Script Editing and Consultation Services:

Diversify your scriptwriting services by offering script editing and consultation. Many content creators and podcasters may have initial scripts but seek professional guidance to enhance them. Providing script editing services ensures that the narrative is polished and impactful. Additionally, offering consultations on script development can position you as a valuable resource for creators seeking narrative expertise.

Monetizing Your Own Podcast or YouTube Channel:

Consider launching your own podcast or YouTube channel as a platform to showcase your scriptwriting skills. This not only serves as a portfolio but also creates an additional income stream through ads, sponsorships, or listener/viewer support. Your own content allows you to demonstrate your storytelling abilities and attract potential clients interested in your scriptwriting services.

Participating in Scriptwriting Competitions:

Many platforms and organizations host scriptwriting competitions that offer cash prizes or opportunities for exposure. Participating in these competitions not only provides a chance to showcase your skills but also potentially opens doors to collaboration with industry professionals or content creators seeking fresh and talented scriptwriters.

Creating Customized Packages for Clients:

When offering scriptwriting services, consider creating customized packages that cater to different needs and budget ranges. This could include options for single scripts, episode bundles, or ongoing scriptwriting services. Providing flexible packages allows you to accommodate various client requirements and increases your appeal to a broader range of content creators.

Staying Updated on Industry Trends:

The landscape of digital content is dynamic, with trends, formats, and audience preferences evolving rapidly. Stay informed about industry trends in video content creation and podcasting. Adapt your scriptwriting style to align with emerging trends, ensuring that your services remain relevant and in demand among content creators and podcasters.

Setting Competitive Rates:

Determining your pricing strategy is crucial in scriptwriting. Research industry standards, consider the complexity of the project, and factor in your level of expertise. While offering competitive rates, emphasize the long-term benefits of engaging scripts in attracting and retaining audiences. Clearly communicate the value of your unique narrative perspective.

Collaborating with Influencers and Industry Experts:

Explore opportunities to collaborate with influencers or industry experts who may require scriptwriting services for their videos or podcasts. These collaborations not only provide exposure to a larger audience but also position you as a scriptwriter capable of working with high-profile clients. Establishing connections with influencers can lead to recurring projects and increased visibility.

Conclusion:

Scriptwriting for videos and podcasts offers a thrilling avenue for talented writers to turn their passion for storytelling into a profitable venture. By identifying opportunities, building a strong portfolio, networking with content creators, and diversifying services, scriptwriters can carve a niche in the dynamic world of digital content creation. Utilize freelance platforms, pitch to potential collaborators, and stay updated on industry trends to ensure that your scriptwriting services remain in demand. As the demand for engaging and narrative-driven content continues to grow, scriptwriters find themselves at the forefront of the creative wave, contributing to the success of digital content creators and podcasters around the globe.

www.ingramcontent.com/pod-product-compliance
Lightning Source LLC
La Vergne TN
LVHW051619050326
832903LV00033B/4580